The Party

Lyrics by Mark Collier
Illustrated by Cesar E. De Castro
Painted by Kathy W. Kim
Designed by Barry K. Haun

© 2001 Little Star Entertainment
  West Covina, California 91791

Published by the Character Building Company
West Covina, California 91791
www.characterbuilding.com
Printed in Korea
ISBN 1-931454-12-4

Library of Congress cataloging-in-publication data is available from the publisher.

Songs in this book are from the **Character Classics** series and are available on cassette and CD. **Coming soon the video series.**

The Party

Habañera from Carmen - Georges Bizet

My dear mama she said to me,
"Tonight we're going to have a big party,
It's important that you behave,
Or you will send me to an early grave!

"Not like last year, you made a mess,
You spilled your dinner on that lady's dress,
Bumped the waiter, he dropped the cake,
And then you brought out Freddy, your pet snake.

"Things will not be the same tonight,
You'll learn some manners, you will be polite,
This year's party will be your last,
Unless you learn a little goodness fast!"

chorus
Will you be good? I will be good!
Will you be good because you know you should?
Will you be good? I will be good!
All right then, very well, it's understood,
You will be good? I will be good,
I will be good because I know I should!
You will be good? Yes, I'll be good,
I will be good, it's understood!

So the people they filled our house,
But I kept quiet as a tiny mouse,
No dropped dinner and no dropped cake,
And most importantly no Fred the Snake.

I was really a model child,
A perfect angel, not my normal wild,
Once was bad, but I made the switch,
And so the party went without a glitch.

Now my mama she knows it's true,
I've learned my lesson, I know what to do,
Next year's party will be the best,
'Cause mama knows I passed the goodness test!

Will you be good? I will be good!
Will you be good because you know you should?
Will you be good? I will be good!
All right then, very well, it's understood,
You will be good? I will be good,
I will be good because I know I should!
You will be good? Yes, I'll be good,
I will be good, it's understood!

You will be good? I will be good,
I will be good because I know I should!
You will be good? Yes, I'll be good!
I will be good, it's understood!

Now *picture this song as you read or sing along...*

My dear mama she said to me,
"Tonight we're going to have a big party,

It's important that you behave,
Or you will send me to an early grave!

Not like last year, you made a mess,
You spilled your dinner on that lady's dress,

Bumped the waiter, he dropped the cake,

And then you brought out Freddy, your pet snake.

Things will not be the same tonight,
You'll learn some manners, you will be polite,

This year's party will be your last,
Unless you learn a little goodness fast!"

All right then, very well, it's understood,

Will you be good?

I will be good!

All right then, very well, it's understood,

You will be good? I will be good,
I will be good because I know I should!

So the people they filled our house,
But I kept quiet as a tiny mouse,

No dropped dinner and no dropped cake,
And most importantly no Fred the Snake.

I was really a model child,
A perfect angel, not my normal wild,

Once was bad,
but I made the switch,
And so the party went
without a glitch.

Now my mama she knows it's true,
I've learned my lesson, I know what to do,

Next year's party will be the best,
'Cause mama knows I passed the goodness test!

Will you be good? I will be good!
Will you be good because you know you should?

Will you be good? I will be good!
All right then, very well, it's understood,

You will be good? I will be good,
I will be good because know I should!

You will be good? Yes, I'll be good,
I will be good, it's understood!

You will be good?

I will be good,

I will be good because I know I should!

Danny's Good Adventure
La Donna e Mobile
Giuseppe Verdi

It was hard to be good
In Danny's neighborhood,
Lots of bad drugs and fights
Crimes almost every night,
But still he'd try his best,
To rise above the rest,
Made it to school each day,
While others stayed away,
Danny heard their bragging,
Put up with their ragging,
He would find a way–
To start a new life!

A new life,
A new life,
To start a new life.
To start a new life.

So Danny studied hard,
And he earned his reward,
Worked at a steady clip,
He won a scholarship,
He always kept in line
Tried to be good and kind,
He became Doctor Dan,
A well-respected man,
He tried hard to be good
And to do what he should.
Danny found a way–
To make a new life!

A new life,
A new life,
To make a new life!
To make a new life!

He tried hard to be good
And to do what he should.
Danny found a way–
To make a new life!

A new life,
A new life,
To make a new life!
To make a new life!

In Your Heart

Piano Sonata No. 8 in C Minor, Op. 13 - Adagio Cantabile
Ludwig van Beethoven

In your heart, that's where all good things start,
Your good thoughts become good words,
Good things you do for others.
Keep it true, the good inside of you,
Protect it and respect it,
Let goodness grow in your heart.

Each day you fill your heart,
Be careful what you put inside it,
Choose the right things, far away from wrong,
Then the good will stay alive inside your heart,

And other people see the good that grows inside of you,
And you can see the good inside of other people, too.

In your heart, that's where all good things start,
Your good thoughts become good words,
Good things you do for others.

Each day you fill your heart,
Be careful what you put inside it,
Choose the right things, far away from wrong,
Then the good will stay alive inside your heart.

In your heart, that's where all good things start,
Your good thoughts become good words,
Good things you do for others.
Keep it true, the good inside of you,
Protect it and respect it,
Let goodness grow in your heart.
Protect it and respect it,
Let goodness grow in your heart.

The Frog on a Log

La Primavera from the Four Seasons

Antonio Vivaldi

Said buzzing bee to the frog,
Who was sitting there on a log,
"Little frog on a log down in the bog
It may be simply a hunch,
But before you eat me for lunch,
There is something you need to know."

Take one little look behind you,
I'm sure that it will remind you,
That you should be good to me,
And maybe the good that you do,
Is finding its way back to you
So will you be good to me?

Said frog to big crocodile,
Who was swimming by with a smile,
"Crocodile with a smile, just wait a while,
I know you're licking your chops,
For a little froggy that hops,
But there's something you need to know."

Take one little look behind you,
I'm sure that it will remind you,
That you should be good to me,
And maybe the good that you do,
Is finding its way back to you
So will you be good to me?

Said the Crocodile to the man,
Hunting crocodiles was his plan,
"Hunting man with a plan, please understand,
But before you do what you do,
And send me off to the zoo,
There is something you need to know."

Take one little look behind you,
I'm sure that it will remind you,
That you should be good to me,
And maybe the good that you do,
Is finding its way back to you
So will you be good to me?

Said hunting man to the bee
Who was buzzing now in the tree,
"I'm allergic to buzzing bees you see,
Before you give me a sting,
And the swelling that it will bring,
There is something you need to know."

Take one little look behind you,
I'm sure that it will remind you,
That you should be good to me,
And maybe the good that you do,
Is finding its way back to you
So will you be good to me?
So will you be good to me?

When Everyone Is Watching

Rondo alla Turca from Piano Sonata in A Major
Wolfgang Amadeus Mozart

Valerie is good, very, very good.
Valerie does everything exactly as she should.
Yes, when everyone is watching her, she's really very good,
Helpful and polite, intelligent and bright,
Valerie is charming, what they call a pure delight.
Yes, she's really quite an angel, that's until she leaves your sight.
When she knows that nobody can see,
Then a different Valerie she'll be.

Now she's not polite, doesn't act so bright,
Valerie's no longer what you call a pure delight,
No, she's really not an angel when she's out of sight.
And you really never, never know,
Is it real or putting on a show?
Is it just a game? Can you be the same?
Why is it that always being good is such a strain?
Don't let all the good things that you do go down the drain!

She is good, she is very good when everyone is watching.
She is bad, very bad when everybody turns away.
Let's be good, let's be very good, when everyone is watching.
Let's be good, better yet, when everybody turns away!

Jeremy is good, very, very good.
Jeremy does everything exactly as he should.
Yes, when everyone is watching him, he's really very good,
Courteous and sweet, really quite a treat,
Jeremy is practically the finest boy you'll meet,
And he seems a perfect angel, but the story's not complete.
When he knows that nobody can see,
Then a different Jeremy he'll be.
Now he's not so sweet, really not a treat,
Jeremy is someone that you wouldn't want to meet.
No, he's not the perfect angel when it's all complete
And you really never ever know,
'Cause he's always putting on a show,
Is it just a game? Can you be the same?
Why is it that always being good is such a strain?
Don't let all the good things that you do go down the drain!

He is good, he is very good when everyone is watching.
He is bad, very bad when everybody turns away.
Let's be good, let's be very good, when everyone is watching.
Let's be good, better yet, when everybody turns away!
Let's be good, better yet, when everybody turns away!

Fine.

fee´-nay
A musical term for the end.